Mark R. Smith

One-Page Business Plan

From Your Vision to Your Success

Contents

1

Introduction

More and more people are making the big decision to start their own business by trying to turn vision into reality. This is not an easy path, to be sure, since it requires a lot of dedication and effort. Analyzing the market, planning your business steps, distributing the budget, and managing the overall business and marketing processes are just a few of the aspects you need to focus on. Hard work will certainly be needed here and, let's be honest, there is still a high risk of failure. What you will be doing during the first months or even the first years of your business is fighting for your place in the market. The obstacles are numerous to be sure. Still, when you achieve your success, the victory will be worth the pain.

Do you think you are among those courageous men and women who are ready to take the risk of starting a new business? If the answer is yes, then you're in the right place. This is a step-by-step guide to help you create the ultimate one-page business plan for your startup which will help you pave your way to success. I know, you might have already thought about the products or services you will offer, but, I would like to show you several important things here that will improve your business vision and add to it. What follows are several things to consider before you actually announce your business to the world.

2

Think Randomly About Random Things: Brainstorm

Whether or not you have already decided what you are going to offer to your target audience and who your target audience is, still brainstorm new ideas. Even big corporations gather their people from time to time to see what new product or service they can offer to their customers and what can be done to improve the customer satisfaction and user experience.

Hence, at the beginning of your endeavor, you need to brainstorm. A lot. If you have a team, then great! Gather your team and think. Even if it's just you, consider things like:

- What you are good at?
- What is each member of the team most passionate about?
- What can you offer to the world that is different compared
- to other similar services or products?
- What will make you look cooler and more fun?
- Who is your target market, customers, buyers, clients?
- When is the best time to let people learn about you?

There are quite a lot of questions to answer. Well, take your time, gather your team together and start brainstorming ideas that create complete answers to all these questions.

As soon as you find out what you want to do, start researching.

Reading about other companies that offer similar products and services is a great place to start since it will help you come up with newer ideas that don't copy what other people have already done. Copying others will hardly bring more customers to you; people will surely require something new and fresh from you. That's why you need to provide them not only with high-quality products and services but also creative solutions to their problems. Your business should deliver something other businesses do not. You must have a solid idea to start with, something that offers solutions to people's problems or meets their needs, otherwise you might lose before you even start. Don't reinvent the wheel, unless you can make a better one.

3

Write A Business Plan

Does it seem like your ideas are going beyond your original scope? Well, that's OK because you will discover even more things in the process of managing your business than you ever did in planning it. Planning is a key factor in establishing a thriving business. A business plan will help you answer more specific questions like:
- What are you going to sell?
- Who are you selling to?
- What are your short-term and long-term goals?
- What do you want your results to look like?
- How will you finance your ideas?
- How much time will you spend on management and other
- aspects of your business?
- Do you need to train your team?
- How many people do you need in your team to make your dream a reality?

Answering these questions will help you understand the specific direction you are taking your company, what expectations you have for your team, and what results you can and can't wait for. Actually, having a good business plan in place may ensure about half the success of your startup. However, you must also ensure its smooth implementation. I promise to come back to this section later on and elaborate in more detail on the different aspects of an awesome business plan.

4

Manage Your Budget

Everything has its price, so starting a business involves finances too. You need to decide how you are going to finance your business costs. Maybe you need to borrow money from a bank or you want to organize a fundraising event (which is quite a trendy thing these days), or maybe you have already got some money put aside after years of working for someone else. Keep in mind, it is important to start a business with at least some money in your pocket. Of course, you can take money from some external sources, but you might need some of your own to cover your personal expenses. It is crucial to keep your personal funds separate from those that must be invested in your startup; otherwise you might end up spending your startup funds and be left without a penny in your pocket.

Although most startups use their own money to start their businesses, they still very often need some external financial assistance depending on the type of business they are starting. For example, if you are a social entrepreneur, it might be easier for you to gather funds through crowdfunding. There are lots of online platforms where you can post a description of your business idea and get help from the people who want to be part of your change initiative.

You can also request a bank loan or a small business loan. There are venture capitalists out there too. These people can help you if you are in need of bigger amounts of money. A larger company may provide you with a few million dollars provided that they have a say in running your company. As you can see, there are several business financing options and it is up to you to decide which one suits you best.

5

Choose The Type Of Business Entity You Will Be

In whatever country you live, if you want to start a new business, you will have to choose a type of legal structure for your business. In the USA, you can choose between a sole proprietorship, a corporation, a partnership, or a limited liability company. You might even need to consult with a business advisor or a lawyer to help you decide which type of business entity suits your business goals. You need to register your business under one legal structure and to help you decide which might be most suitable for you, let us now briefly discuss all of them:

Sole proprietorship

If you do not have a team, and you are going to own your business by yourself, then you might want to be responsible for it all on your own. In this case, you might consider choosing a sole proprietorship. You might pay lower taxes in this type of business, but at the same time, you will be the only person liable for the debts and responsibilities of your business.

Partnership

In a partnership, two or more people are legally liable for the business. This type of business structure is very much like the sole proprietorship. The only difference is the number of people involved. In the first case, only one individual is liable for all the debts and obligations of the business. In the case of a partnership, two or more people are liable.

Corporation

If you do not want to be held liable for your company's debts personally, you might want to choose the business type known as a corporation. This will make your company liable for all debts. Corporations can do a variety of things; such as pay taxes, sign contracts, sue or be sued etc. There are C and S types of corporations. With an S type, the owner is only taxed on a personal level.

Limited Liability Company (LLC)

You might have heard about LLCs before. Many startups choose to take on this type of business structure. This legal structure is kind of a mix between a corporation and a partnership since the company becomes liable for the debts and responsibilities, while the tax benefits are very similar to those of a partnership.

It is up to you to decide which option to choose. Bear in your mind that a business structure always affects the way you pay your taxes, or the way you or your company are liable in case something goes wrong. This is another question that must be given proper consideration to avoid possible headaches later on. After you choose a legal structure for your business, you should register it with the government and the Internal Revenue Service (IRS).

6

Find The Right Team

Most successful startups have the coolest teams. And, if you are not going to be the only employee of your business, then most probably you need a team. Usually, bright ideas have the power to gather bright people around them, so you might already have a great team to support you. If you are still in search of yours, these tips will surely be helpful.

Start hiring creatively

Of course, recruiters and HR specialists might be of great help when it comes to choosing the right candidate for the positions your company offers. However, you could try to do it all yourself and to spice your selection process with the creativity that usually defines startups. Your ideas are assumed to be unique, so your people should be unique too. That's why it's a good idea to try experimenting while interviewing the job candidates. You can also use your professional network or LinkedIn to find the best team players for your startup.

Also, feel free to offer your candidates some tricky puzzles or problem-solving games and exercises. This is a bit unorthodox but it will help you understand the way your candidates think. Try putting them into stressful situations to see which solutions and ideas they will come up with. Some companies offer candidates sample work or ask them to solve problems within a given amount of time. By doing this you will be able to choose the brightest men and women to join your team.

Give your people time to become part of your culture

As soon as you have found the right candidate for the job, give them a probation period for both of you to get to know each other better. In a lot of ways, getting a good employee is like getting to know a good friend. Usually, such an adjustment period lasts from 1–3 months. You might have some office/company rules or guidelines in place that you expect to be followed, so let the newcomer learn about these rules. You do not need identically cloned employees; you need team players who are committed to your company's vision. So let people take time to get used to your company's culture. Then, observe their work and see whether they really are the people your company needs or if you should keep on searching for the right match.

Check whether your people are ready to learn

As an employer, you must provide your employees with the chance to learn and expand their knowledge of what they do. As an employee, each of your team players must be willing to learn otherwise your startup will become stagnant, and fail. So, take care to hire people who get excited about learning something new and of expanding their experience. These will be the people who will later on back your business endeavors.

As soon as you hire the right people, make sure you create the necessary bonds between them. It is your task to make them a team since they might be very different from one another. Here are a few things you should be prepared to do as a boss:
- Let your people ask you questions on a daily basis
- Meet them outside the workplace
- Be a role model for them
- Let them have fun in the workplace, praise them and give them

bonuses

You can have a great idea, but you need great people with you in order to make your vision a reality. Make sure you include this point in your business strategy!

7

Brand Your Startup And Start Marketing It

A whole book could be written on how to brand a business and how to place it wisely in the market. Here, I'm going to give you a quick overview of the most basic branding factors to consider when starting a new business. First of all, the packaging (both literally and figuratively) of your product or service should be attractive. In other words, even the greatest idea should be branded so that people can readily identify it. Imagine Nike without their swoosh or Pepsi without their red, white, and blue logo. Would they be as successful? The answer is no. Of course, you should never underestimate the power of word-of-mouth advertising but your relatives and team-mates are not enough to spread the word about your business.

The branding must start long before you actually launch your products or services. Your audience must be ready to instantly buy whatever you offer long before you start offering it. You might wonder how this can even be possible if people have never experienced your products or services. That's a fair question. Let me explain.

Company name, tagline, and logo

You have two options here. Either you pay some branding company to create this for you or you do it all on your own. As a startup, you might want to research a bit and do it yourself. To start, take a look at what other similar brands have:

- What do their logos look like?
- What do their taglines and slogans look like?
- How unique are they?
- How do these brands interact with their customers?

It is important to observe all these things in order to not copy other businesses and make your brand even cooler and way more original.
- As for the company name, make sure it is something that describes you best of all. Follow these tips to make your company name stand out as much as possible:
- Keep it short and memorable
- Make it related to what you offer
- Let it describe your vision
- Make sure it is understandable for your target market
- Do not be afraid of experimenting; for example, you can even invent a name for your brand
- Make it related to what you offer
- Let it describe your vision
- Make sure it is understandable for your target market
- Do not be afraid of experimenting; for example, you can even invent a name for your brand

Another important thing that will help you tell your story is your company tagline/slogan. Usually, this is either a phrase or a short sentence. However, it is ridiculously hard to be brief when it comes to representing a whole company with a simple sentence. You might need the help of a copyrighter to generate a worthy slogan for your brand. If you decide to create it yourself, bear these tips in mind:
- Include a keyword or a key benefit your company offers
- Make it memorable
- Make it fun and easygoing
- Let it be something motivational rather than intriguing

As soon as you have chosen a company name and a tagline, it is time to create a logo that is going to represent your company virtually everywhere since it will be on your business cards, your packaging and even on your website. A logo is the first visual that reaches your customer and tells them about your company. So, it should be closely connected with the company name (some startups even choose their logos to be the stylized textual version of their company names) and, of course, it should be catchy and interesting to look at. Usually, when creating a logo, companies put some internal meaning into it. For example, let's take Toyota's well-known logo. It represents all the letters in the word Toyota with one simple symbol. Examples are endless; you can search them on the web or you can simply hire a freelance designer to create a few samples for you. If you wonder where you can find freelancers, UpWork and Fiverr are the best platforms to find and hire some really talented men and women ready to work on one-time projects at really low prices.

Company website and social media presence

A company website is practically a must-have for any business. It will help your customers get in touch with you and know you better. Usually, the website's domain name is the same as the company's name since it helps the brand get easily recognized. As for the website itself, make it as responsive and user-friendly as possible. The navigation should be intuitive and simple. Make sure the design matches your overall brand identity and your business voice.

A website is not a one-time thing, remember. You can't just create one and leave it be. It must be updated constantly with useful, interesting, and engaging content. You had better have a "blog posts" page that allows you to post interesting stuff either about your products and services, or your company news and announcements or your daily routine. It is a good idea to show the world what an awesome team you are since it will motivate people towards buying things from you.

An ideal website must have the following sections plus some additional ones depending on your business goals:

- An "About us" page where you tell the website visitor about your team, your services, your vision, your daily routine and the people you work for
- A separate "Services or Products" page where you show in more detail what you do (you can also add price packages for each service or product you provide)
- A blog as mentioned above
- A "Contact us" page that must include your contact information, addresses, phone numbers and the rest

A website is not enough for your media presence. You need to be active in social media as well. Open your company accounts in Facebook, Twitter, LinkedIn, Instagram, Reddit, Flickr, and Pinterest. Make sure you have a YouTube account as well to post company videos. All these social media websites will help you get in touch with your potential customers and enlarge your customer base by providing them with useful information and fun videos. You can even offer your followers special coupons and discounts. A good social reputation will help preserve a good brand image that everyone wants to follow and be a part of.

Besides, social media platforms help companies create long-lasting brand-customer relationships. By being active in social media, you will be able to see what people think about your brand and your services. This will help you improve whatever you are selling.

Your customer service and your employees

Your marketing efforts must be backed with perfect customer service. Your brand should be consistent in delivering what it promises.

Moreover, every employee of yours (regardless of their role in the team) must acknowledge that their work impacts your brand's image directly. Following are several simple tips for you:

- Create a company "voice" and stick to it
- Use consistent design
- Keep true to your vision
- Always keep your promises

And remember, make sure your products are easy and intuitive to use. Whether it is product packaging or a website interface, it should provide a simple and easy user experience. These are several things you must consider when starting a new business. As soon as you have an awesome idea, it is time to generate a business plan.

8

What Is A Business Plan?

A business plan is a simple roadmap that outlines the steps you are going to take to transform your business goals and vision into reality.It is a document that reflects how you and your team are going to achieve your business goals.

In the past, a business plan was usually a long and boring formal document that had to be written and put aside on a shelf along with volumes of books that nobody was going to read. Today, it has transformed into something much more useful and effective, something you cannot just write up and ignore. A business plan might be needed for different reasons such as:

- Finding investors
- Requesting a loan
- Guiding your employees towards the realization of company goals
- Tracking business progress
- Managing assets and finances

However, the most important reason for creating a business plan is to ensure you follow the right steps when starting your business. It is a kind of guide that will help you achieve success and take into account all the details of starting your business. When you write a business plan just for yourself, you can omit the following things:

- The description of the management team

- The description of how you are going to close the business in case your initiative fails

This means that a modern business plan does not have to be a long document. There was a time when business plans were easily more than 40-50 pages. Nowadays, you can even have a one-page simple and persuasive business plan that meets all your business needs.

As you can see, a business plan is nothing more than a simple draft of how you are going to succeed in your business. The business plan is not a tricky and complicated document like you might have imagined. Instead, it is something really useful whether you are starting a new business or running an existing one. Following are a few ideas to help you get the idea of what a business plan really is:
- Typically, it is not something too long (even one page can suffice)
- For most successful businesses it is just a few bullet points on a piece of paper
- It usually includes your business goals, the tasks you are going to complete to achieve them and a few ideas about how you are going to distribute your funds
- You only need to print out a business plan in case it is needed for outsiders (banks, investors) to decide whether to provide you with financial assistance or not

9

Who Needs A Business Plan?

Most importantly, it's not just startups who need business plans but also existing businesses since they might need to make adjustments to their business plans based on economic situations. Thus, startups can benefit from a business plan by finding investors, and existing businesses can benefit from one by finding new ways to grow themselves into larger entities. In other words, if you take your business seriously, then you really NEED a business plan.

Startups need them

Following are the brief reasons why startups need a business plan. A startup needs a business
- To setup budget and business milestones
- To setup deadlines for the milestones to be completed
- To convince venture capitalists and other investors to invest in their project

Existing businesses need them

A running business needs a business plan:
- To address changes resulting from changing economic situations

in the world
- To find new opportunities to grow
- To manage overall goals and team responsibilities as well as monitor resources and successes in order to be competitive enough in the market

10

What Are The Benefits Of A Business Plan?

We have identified what a business plan is and who needs it. Let us now see what benefits it provides to businessmen and startups in general:

Helps To Get Funded

Potential investors will be most likely to invest in a business that has a valid business plan. A good business plan will provide them with the necessary answers to their questions and will increase the chances of a business getting funded.

Every investor wants to know:
- Why should they invest in your business over others?
- Why will people need your products and services and how likely will they be to buy from you?
- What makes you better from other similar businesses?

A good business plan must give answers to all these questions. It must motivate the investors towards trusting you and believing in you.

Helps to manage cash flow

Let's imagine you have already been funded. Congrats! So, what's next? Your next step must be generating an overview of how you are going to spend the funds. You cannot afford to mismanage your funds since they are not for your whole life. You need to calculate what assets you are going to purchase, what they will cost, how much you are going to spend on every asset you get, how you much money you are going to pay for your possible debts, what taxes you must pay and etc.

Decreases your legal risks

As mentioned above, you must first of all choose a type of business legal structure that fits your needs. A well-written business plan will help you understand which legal structure is the most suitable for you. As a result, you will be able to avoid penalties or fines. If you feel you cannot choose a business legal structure on your own, you can hire a business advisor.

Helps to have everything under control

Planning and re-planning is necessary to be able to control all the business processes. You might have millions of strategies to consider and hundreds of techniques to use in order to achieve your goals and to complete your milestones. However, you cannot do everything all at once. Instead, you need a clear and understandable strategy to follow on a long-term basis. Once written down, a strategy will help you omit all the other possible solutions to the problems and concentrate on one particular solution instead. As a result, you will be able to do the following:
- Stick to the strategy you and your team have chosen
- Define specific, measureable goals and try to achieve them through hard work
- Set priorities more objectively
- Understand the links and interdependencies between your milestones
- Track your team's progress

- Better delegate your purposes and ideas
- Manage your team in a more productive manner since you will know who does what, how, and when

Helps to avoid problems

Overall, the main idea of having a business plan is to avoid problems when implementing your business strategy. While researching costs, your startuper rights, licensing and taxation, you might find out that your preliminary assumptions were wrong. That's why one needs a business plan to be able to make more refined and mature business decisions, and to avoid further problems and headaches.

Provides you with ideas on what to do at the end

When starting a business, you might have a plan A, plan B, and even a plan C to carry out your initiative. However, not everything goes well all the time; some startup ideas do fail. If the unthinkable happens, what will you do about it? Having an exit strategy is not a must-have in a business plan. However, it is a plus to have one since an exit plan will help you look at things from a more realistic perspective. You had better make proper calculations right at the beginning of it all in order to avoid bankruptcy at the end. A good exit strategy might help you sell your business at the right moment or let you save the last of your money instead of making unnecessary purchases.

These are the benefits that a well-written business plan can provide you with. Let us now take a look at what the most common types of business plans are and which one to choose for your company.

11

Common Types Of Business Plans

Business plans can be of different types depending on your needs and goals. One startup might need the so-called strategic plan while another person might need a one-page business plan. Knowing the differences between them will help you make the right choices and plan your business successfully. Let us look at the most common types of business plans and see what each of them is all about:

Standard business plan

The standard business plan can either be a printed document or one posted online. Usually, you need a standard plan for a presentation event such as when introducing the business to your partners, clients, potential investors or loan specialists. Such a plan usually starts with an executive summary which is meant to introduce the main aspects of your business.

The standard business plan usually includes the following sections:
· Executive summary
· Company overview
· Product and/or service description
· The target audience
· Goals, milestones, and implementation strategy
· The management team

- The financial aspect
- Analysis
- Additional documents

These chapters or sections of a standard business plan can be placed in a different order based on your need and preferences. However, make sure to include all of them since the investors and the loan specialists will be looking forward to seeing them all during your presentation. Also, you might need a more detailed document on the financial aspect of your business. An appendix with the analysis of cash flow might be quite useful here.

Lean business plan

A lean business plan is more for your team than a group of investors or loan specialists. This type of plan can be used to remind you of your milestones, goals, and deadlines. The lean business plan usually includes the following 4 chapters:

1. **Strategy overview** includes your market description, the product or service you are offering to your potential customers, and your long-term milestones
2. **Strategy execution** states how you are going to achieve your goals and what methods you are going to use
3. **Specifications** tell you about particular milestones, responsibilities of team members, and the numbers to track
4. **Cash flow** must include how much you are going to spend on materials, human resources and other assets and how you are going to distribute the funds

A lean business plan is sometimes also referred to as an **internal plan** since it reflects the needs and objectives of the people INSIDE the company and is written more like a to-do list for them.

Operations business plan

This plan is also known as an **annual plan** and it is very much like the lean business plan. The main similarity is that it also accentuates the milestones that must be implemented by the management team, as well as the deadlines that must be met during the course of work. An operations plan is mainly needed to track the company progress. Because of this it is useful both for startups and for existing businesses. An operations business plan can be updated once a year to meet your changing business needs.

Startup business plan

The name already implies that this type of a business plan is meant for startups only. Usually, a startup business plan is very much like the lean business plan. However, depending on the financing options, it may include a detailed description regarding the cash flow. The startups need to know how much funds they are going to spend on their website, graphics, logo design, office equipment and etc. Usually, these are one-time expenses that are not repeated for a long period of time since, for example, no one is going to change a website every two months. In this respect, startups need to calculate their initial expenses in more detail.

Also, if you are going to show your startup plan to an outsider, it's a good idea to include the following aspects (no need to go too deep though):
- An executive summary
- Company overview and management team
- Market description
- Marketing plan and product plan
- Probable expenses and costs

Feasibility plan

A feasibility plan is usually needed to see whether an idea has a chance to work well in the market. Thus, it is used to validate an idea, a product, or a service and to see whether it can bring profit or not. Two main questions are answered with this plan:
1. Who will purchase the product/service?
2. Will the purchase rates ensure proper profit?

As you can see, feasibility plans do not usually include the full range of chapters normally included in standard or lean business plans. Instead, they include recommendations and advice regarding the business strategy, techniques, and methods.

Expansion business plan

An expansion or a **growth business plan** is usually meant for existing businesses that want to enlarge the production of a specific product or to increase the volumes of sales. You can plan the expansion of a particular area of your business by using the expansion plan. Depending on the financial aspect of your initiative, you might need either a brief or a detailed description of your expenses, costs of materials and other assets needed to conduct an expansion of a service. If you do not need outside investments, then you might just skip this part and concentrate on the business strategy in more detail.

Strategic business plan

This is a type of a business plan that will help you see the big picture. Usually, a strategic plan concentrates more on the sales and promotion tactics rather than financial projections. Therefore, it includes a lot of description and explanation regarding team management and implementation of different strategies.

A strategic business plan is more about helping you choose what you are good at or what your strengths are. As time passes, you might need to lean on your strengths rather than experiment with vague tactics and procedures. As a result, a strategic plan will help you understand which aspects of your business will bring you more benefits and more profit, of course. As soon as you decide who is going to do what, you will be able to schedule your milestones and objectives correctly. The proper and timely implementation of your ideas will surely lead to success.

One-page business plan

This is the last and maybe the most interesting type of a business plan since it can be useful for virtually everyone: investors, banks, vendors, and employees. That's the reason why a one-page business plan is sometimes referred to as a **business pitch document**. It is simple, brief, comprehensive and understandable. You need not resize the fonts to fit your writing into one page. Instead, you just really need to write a summary of your business. There is no need to add tons of information, graphs, and pictures, or useless sentences since everything must be clear and concise in this document. Such a plan can serve many purposes and the two most important ones are the following:

- You can see the whole idea in one sheet and you can make adjustments whenever needed
- You can introduce your business to outsiders in a simple manner

As a startup, you are free to choose any of the aforementioned types of business plans. Usually, it is a good idea to start with the one-page plan since it doesn't take too much time and effort to generate one. Later on, as soon as you refine your ideas and expectations from you team, you can move on to more complex types of business plans.

12

What To Include In A One-Page Business Plan?

We have just reviewed several most common types of business plans. Now, let's see what elements or sections should be included in virtually any business plan. Note that we will be discussing many aspects of a one-page business plan. You won't need every one. Or, maybe you will. It's up to you to include or to omit any aspect. The descriptions of sections will be as detailed as possible. Still, you need not turn your business plan into a thick book. Remember, this information is only meant to help you when generating your own business plan. Your plan does not necessarily have to be very long. Following are the sections of a business plan:

1. Executive summary
2. Company overview
3. Description of products and services
4. Target market analysis
5. Strategy, implementation, and success measurement metrics
6. Management team
7. The financial aspect

These are the core chapters to be included in your business plan. You can merge them or split them depending on your needs. Also, if you are going to introduce your business to outsiders, make sure you add a nice cover page to your business plan. Company name, logo, tagline and, contact information must be included here. All this should be done to ensure that your business plan looks professional. Investors and vendors take details into consideration, so take your time to make your business plan as attractive as possible. Now, let us continue with the main sections of a business plan and see what each of them is all about:

Executive summary

The first impression must be good enough to make potential investors follow up with the rest. Hence, an executive summary must be as attractive as possible. Keep it short, engaging, fun, informative, and even intriguing. Most vendors and loan providers will not make it till the end if you offer them a poorly-written, vague or boring executive summary. Think of it as something that must motivate and compel your audience.

Since most startups offer a solution to a problem, the executive summary of your startup's business plan must contain precise information about the solution you offer. Thus, feel free to include the following points there:
- The problem and the solution you offer
- The ways you are going to implement the solution
- Who is going to do what and in what time frame?
- How much money do you need to carry out your plan?
- What will the results look like?

Of course, it is difficult to convey all the answers to these questions in one simple section. Still, you need to be brief, informative and compelling at the same time. I would also suggest writing this section last, i.e. you must finish with all the sections of a business plan and only then start writing the executive summary so that you do not miss a thing. After reading your executive summary, your audience should not feel like crumpling it up and throwing it away!

Company overview

If you opt for a one-page business plan, then this section might need to be made really short. We have already discussed the main legal structures that a business can have. In this section, you need to mention which legal structure your business falls under; whether it is a sole proprietorship, a partnership, a limited liability company or a corporation (either C or S type). Your investors might need this information to see who is going to be held liable for your company's debts and responsibilities.

The company overview must also include information about the sector your business falls into. For example, you must tell them whether it is going to be in the sector of retail, food service, textile industry, hospitality, manufacturing or something else. You can also include information about whether yours is a startup or an existing business.

Description of products and services

This might be the most interesting part of your business plan for outsiders since it is about what you are going to offer to the people that is new and exciting. In the description of your products and services, you should tell your audience what to expect from you and what you are going to achieve.

Your startup offers a solution to a problem. Make sure you introduce the problem properly and then continue with the solution your team offers. You must convince the investors that your solution is the best among other similar solutions and that you are competitive enough to hit the market with a worthy innovation.

Following are a few tips for you for writing a great product and service description:

- Tell your audience about the technology, hardware or software you are using to deliver your services
- Enumerate the core factors that help build your products
- Explain how people will be using your products and services
- Think as if you are the customer to be better able to list the benefits your products/services offer
- Don't stress the product's or service's features but the benefits your customer will get if they acquire it
- Include the prices of your products and services
- Include information about what makes your product or service stand out from the bunch of similar things that already exist in the market
- Explain why your products and services will bring profit to the investors

Try to be super-accurate when providing numbers and facts. Investors like hard facts, so provide them with some. Make this section as understandable as possible so that no one has any additional questions after reading it.

Target market analysis

As mentioned above, your business will be trying to solve a problem. It is, of course, super-cool. However, ask yourself whether you are going to solve the problem for the entire world. I do not think so, unless your product or service is really outstanding. Instead, we are speaking about a smaller, yet still awesome idea that is going to solve the problem of a target market such as a particular group of people. You need to specify who that market is. For example, if you are going to sell summer skirts of different colors, then most probably your target market/audience includes mostly women who are likely to buy those skirts during summer months. Understanding whom you are going to sell your products and services to is crucial for building your promotional and marketing strategies.

As a result, you need to not only know about your target market but also about what they are looking for, what they will need in the near future, and how they might change over time.

In this section, you need to do the following things:

- Understand who is going to purchase from you
- See what your target audience needs
- Find out how much money they are ready to spend on your products and services
- Explore how often your products and services might be needed by the target market
- Find out how you can find them and reach out to them
- See what your competitors do to deliver similar services to the same target market

This information will provide you with ideas on how to behave in the market. Also, proper market research will help you make decisions regarding the pricing, distribution, and advertisement of your products and services. Defining the market means identifying its gender, age, demographics, size, structure, and behaviors. Based on this information, you will be able to calculate what the prices of your products and services will be, who your competitors are, how you are going to compete with them, what you can offer to your customers that is new, why the target market is going to prefer your products and services over those offered by other service providers and so on.

Strategy, implementation and success measurement metrics

As soon as you identify your target market, you can start building a strategy to reach that market. This section of your business plan must include the answers to the following questions:

- How are you going to promote your products and services?
- What kind of sales tactics you are going to implement?
- What should be the deadlines of each milestone to be completed?
- Who will be responsible for what?
- What tools you are going to use to measure success?

It is crucial to not only generate a marketing strategy but also to measure your success. For example, if you have set a milestone of reaching 1000 visitors per month for your newly-established website, then you can use visitor tracking tools to see whether you really achieve this milestone or not. This is just one example of setting a goal and checking its completion. You should include all your marketing tactics in this section to look more compelling and professional in the eyes of potential investors.

In this section, you can also include information about the technology and facilities you are going to use in order to implement your business strategy. Maybe you need some special equipment or a special place/location in order to get started.

Management team

If you are intending to have a one-page business plan, then you might not need to include this section unless you do not have to show it to an investor. Usually, this section includes information about each member of the management team. Short biographies are included to show the potential investors that a well-trained and experienced staff is going to work on the startup. Make sure you attach full-length CVs to the document.

Also, this section can comprise information about the founder(s) of the company, the people who had the bright idea to start a business, and where it all started. People might also want to know where your business is registered, where your office is situated and how many employees you have or are going to employ in the future.

The financial aspect

It would be really hard to start a business without any money in your pocket. And if you are going to search for investors for your startup, then you must show them your projections regarding your finances. This section of your business plan should highlight the amount of money you need to launch your startup. Several calculations and even tables might be needed to make the information easier to comprehend. You can include the following information:
- Costs for acquiring hardware and software
- Funds needed to pay the personnel for the first few months
- Funds needed to acquire other assets required to implement the business strategy
- Costs for advertisement and promotion

You will also need to include the following things in this section:
- Income statement
- Cash flow
- Balance sheet

If these terms sound too odd to you, you might need to consult an accountant before putting finance-related information into your business plan. However, this does not mean that the analysis should be long and boring. Make sure it is brief and smoothly-written instead. Choose the most important points to emphasize and leave out unnecessary details.

These are the main sections to include in your business plan. Still, if you want to build a one-page business plan, you can omit several of them and instead focus on just the necessary ones. Remember that startups that have a business plan in place have a greater chance at success. At the same time, you should note that just writing a business plan does not guarantee success. By all means, you should work hard to implement it and to complete your goals. Sometimes, a business plan might need changes in order to better serve you. Don't be afraid of making appropriate adjustments to it. View your business plan both as a tool that can ensure investment in your business and as a tool that can help you in daily management of your team and the implementation of your marketing strategy.

Following is a sample one-page business plan. You can use it when creating your own version. Hopefully, this guide will help you turn your vision into reality and to achieve success. If you have already launched your own business, then feel free to share your experiences with us. Do not forget to share this article with your friends and colleagues. Good luck in turning your dreams into your reality!

13

One-Page Business Plan Template

Logo
  Company name:
  Tagline:
  Contacts (address, website, telephone number):

Company overview

Type of legal structure:

Mission statement:

Business sector:

Products and services

Short description of products and services:

Prices of each product and service:

Benefits of the products and services:

Target market analysis

Description of the target market:

Business growth goals:

Strategy, implementation and success measurement metrics

Description of sales tactics:

Milestones and deadlines:

Description of promotion tactics:

Several measurement metrics:

The financial aspect

Income projection and explanation:

Expenses (website hosting, facilities, equipment etc.):

Costs and salaries:

Thanks

Thank you for reading One-Page Business Plan: From Your Vision to Your Success. If you enjoy this book, please consider leaving a short review on Amazon or Goodreads, and share it with your friends. As always, your support encourages and motivates me to write more for you.

About The Author

CEO and Founder of E-Finance Solutions Mark Smith, has more than 20 years of experience directing progressive start-up firms with revenues exceeding 50 million. Mark has lead E-Finance for over 10 years, directing over 5,000 employees for his cutting-edge financial software system. E-Finance has a global client base, and is steadily growing worldwide. Mark believes innovation, drive and recruiting a talented diverse workforce are the key components to his companies' success.

With a strong financial and technology background, Mark has spent previous years working in banking and Fortune 500 companies as a software developer. His strong multifaceted experience in investing, accounting, resource allocation, computer programming and software development has led to the creation of the latest financial software technology. E-Finance Solutions is ranked as one of the best companies to work for in the U.S. due to their employee focused culture. His understanding and belief in e-marketing channels, innovation, people-centred organizations and development of user-friendly cost-effective software for large and small business needs have put him on a constant path of growth. Mark has an MBA from Stanford University with a concentration in finance where he graduated with honours. Also, he holds a BSc in Computer Science from MIT, where he was treasurer of The Technology Inventors Club. Currently, he is on the Board of Directors for Young Girl Coders, where young girls and female adolescents are encouraged to develop their technology skills. The generosity continues, as Mark regularly speaks to young female students at schools about entrepreneurship, and future jobs in technology and software.

Made in the USA
Middletown, DE
15 October 2017